The Elegy on Hats

ALSO BY STEPHEN BERG

POETRY AND PROSE POETRY

Bearing Weapons
The Queen's Triangle
The Daughters
Nothing in the Word: Versions of Aztec songs
Clouded Sky by Miklos Radnoti (with Steven Polgar and S. J. Marks)
Grief: Poems & Versions of Poems
Oedipus The King (with Diskin Clay)
With Akhmatova at the Black Gates
Sea Ice: Versions of Eskimo Songs
In It
Home to the afterlife
Crow with No Mouth: Ikkyū
New & Selected Poems
Sleeping Woman (public art project with the painter Tom Chimes)
The Steel Cricket: Versions 1958-1997
Oblivion
Shaving
Porno Diva Numero Uno
Halo
Footnotes to an Unfinished Poem
X=
Rimbaud: Versions & Inventions

ANTHOLOGIES

Naked Poetry (with Robert Mezey)
Between People (with S. J. Marks and J. Michael Pilz)
About Women (with S. J. Marks)
In Praise of What Persists
Singular Voices
The Body Electric (with David Bonanno & Arthur Vogelsang)
My Business is Circumference

The Elegy on Hats

STEPHEN BERG

THE SHEEP MEADOW PRESS
RIVERDALE-ON-HUDSON, NEW YORK

All inquiries and permission requests should be addressed to:
The Sheep Meadow Press, P.O. Box 1345
Riverdale-on-Hudson, NY 10471

Design: Eileen Neff
Typeset by The Sheep Meadow Press
Distributed by The University Press of New England

Printed on acid-free paper in the United States. This book meets the guidelines for permanence and durability of the Committee on Production Guidelines for Book Longevity of the Council on Library Resources.

The Library of Congress Cataloging-in-Publication Data

Berg, Stephen.
The elegy on hats / Stephen Berg.
    p. cm.
ISBN 1-931357-95-1 (pbk. : alk. paper)
I. Title.

PS3552.E7E46 2005
811'.6--dc22

2005002852

Special thanks to The Daniel W. Dietrich Foundation for a grant that made possible the design of this book.

To my dear friend Jerry Shestack

"My humiliations have been graces from God."

"Nothing upon the earth is interesting except religions."

—Charles Baudelaire

The Elegy on Hats

1.

This poem never written by Baudelaire
listed under [E] in his [Plans and Notes]

was never written not because he died
was never written not because he lied

to his mother about sex drugs money
especially money Baudelaire had

millions of francs stashed in a secret drawer
he had built into a walnut armoire

royalties he made under a pseudonym
from a translation of Hamlet also

Oedipus under the same fake name
Francois Thames nevertheless he still wrote

that crazy bitch for money wailed begged her
to send him rent enough for food a new

black silk top hat for the opera then too
he needed contact with the ghost of himself

in female form with the one who bore him
nursed him screwed up his mind he needed

"the absolute security of childhood"
according to Sartre quoting CB

in a letter to his mother "I was
always living in you" did he ever

mature to distinguish himself from her
was that his *volupté* the ridiculed

self whose audience is always the one
self he knew he should be but could not be

once when he was drunk out walking he tried
to masturbate onto a tree trunk screaming

and I translate "God wanted me to be
a whore who worshipped Him who sucked His cock"

Paris nights his mistress would drag him home
as always the self-consciousness of being

alone with one person bearing the weight of
consciousness unexplained how could it be

nevermore it may be true that Baudelaire
attained Ikkyū's "floating cloud of the body"

without knowing it since the impasse
of his life he realized was impossible

to break through he knew so he embraced it
he could not be alone he could not love

or how he loved he could not believe was
what others thought love was thus the mirror

not the other but oneself as the other lived
that worst of hells that interior hell

in "To Each His Monster" where he pins down
every man's fate "Each of them bore on his back

an enormous Monster heavy as
a sack of flour or coal or the para-

phernalia of a Roman footsoldier
but the chimerical beast was not

an immobile mass on the contrary
it enveloped and oppressed each man

with its powerful elastic muscles
it clung with two enormous claws to its bearer's

chest and its bright grotesque head rose above
the man's brow like one of those horrendous

helmets with which the warriors of antiquity
hoped to increase their enemy's terror"

which reminds me of myself and perhaps you
"I am Life unbearable implacable Life!"

referring to the slavery of Time
why care about Baudelaire my wild fate

has been to act as if I were somebody else
without knowing it until the agony

of disaster held up its black mirror to me
it's okay to let things be they are them-

selves as we are us a nothingness a
vile beauty of incompleteness which

refuses to be itself consciously
can't you just let the silence be what it is

3

no but *I'm no good with women* haunts me
ejected like a plume of white excrement

those words who uttered them I don't know or how
to narrate the story of. . . maybe I should

start with my mother maybe all stories
should start there since I (and you) started there

I remember she told me once that when
her brother died of TB the insanity

she felt drove her to ask people on the street
who she was *Will I die?* she must have howled

help me help me help but there was no help
was I alive then I don't know never

got the dates straight I think I was I think
she strove like a demon all her life not to

commit suicide and she succeeded
by concentrating on things like knitting

a penis-shaped wool warmer red and blue
for my father's cock that had a pouch too

to hold his balls at U of P football games
by collecting antique glass beads weird though

I can barely say what she was like the essence
of a person the "who" can you describe it

in physical terms images or is
there no such thing as essence only acts

4

and words and the mostly hidden causes
of those acts those words it's what made her

Hilda Berg that I wish I could locate
what she and I were "She injected

her insanity into you" a doctor
once said to me "Why did she hate me so much?"

I asked him "Because you exist" he said
the words were a spike hammered into my brain

he was right so for me to exist has
been impossible to take for granted

better yet nearly impossible at all
not in the sense of a gift a mistake

or bad joke every day I have felt
uneasy about being here afraid

of being who I am as if it were
an insult an arrogant assumption

based on nothing factual insouciant
to hear myself saying this now unsure

of whether I actually believe it
"I sing of calamitous dogs" warbled

the ruined French poet and I understand
what he meant in my own way my mother

used to coo love words at her miniature white
long-haired Chinese dog GiGi then the next

moment scream at it with violent hatred
even though the dog had done nothing bad

"Two rungs above a dog" the doctor said
was where I was in her eyes oh the truth

nothing like it to make this crazed Jew smile
but such truth for me is like a fantasy

I believe is both real and not real are
calamitous dogs possible are they

have you ever seen one "dance on the
terrified grass" or sensed one's nose sniffing

your asshole I associate the phrase
"the tyranny of the human face"

with such canines the face below each hat
on any head my mother collected

hats hundreds of them some found in thrift shops
some bought on sale at Bendels Saks Duskins

Christ two entire closets she had stacked up
with rows of hats one on top of another

I'll never forget the first time I came home
from college and opened the hall closet

and the closet in her bedroom so many
hats black shiny straw silk fur narrow brim

looking at them all I could think of was
the guillotine how one absolutely

needed a head to wear a hat unless
of course you tied the decapitated

prisoner to a stake or pole and stuck
a hat on the stump of his hemorrhaging neck

hundreds of headless hats moss green felt
fedora-like mannish hat wide snap brim

weightless white Panama sunhat fishing hat
covered with fake decorative trout flies

and all those invisible heads "neither
attached nor detached" listening to my list

watching me from somewhere else behold hats
like divine relics left behind by dead

courtesans queens fashion models obsessed
women afraid to bare their heads outdoors

who even wore hats to bed fucked sucked
wearing a hat ate dinner in a hat

breakfast lunch were driven insane by hats'
power to suggest some universal

world-shaking secret truth that would reveal
the meaning of life why we are here what

we should do and how and when and money
how to make a lot fast how to resolve

our "inner muteness" and meet with an "un-
known self" enter "that inner place where things churn"

7

where hats are like the surprise of suddenly
knowing a truth one always knew but refused

to believe I'd open those two closets
when no one was in the house stand there

run my eyes up and down the silent rows
three deep at least seven feet high reach out

and stroke one then another enjoy the lush
texture of cashmere cool faille raw silk

feathers and lace her hats were becoming
more than hats other than hats holy

epiphanies whose meanings slipped away
I think my mother kept herself alive

by collecting hats finding new ones lived
an endless quest for the absolute hat

that would eliminate the need for needing
anything I believe unquestionably

too that walking down the street thinking about
her hats allayed the boiling anxiety

that scarred her mind those seductive fables
or myths of headlessness (whatever that

could have meant to her) were a great comfort
why else would Baudelaire have planned to write

their elegy his mother's and my mother's
twin objects of desire catastrophic

dog-like inescapable famished fates
where every man begins to speak of love

is impossible like the "unconnected
monologue of the patient on one side

and the almost absolute silence of
the psychiatrist on the other—a

great methodological principle
invented by Freud" or Mahler's "The most

important thing in music is not
in the score" she was (*my* mother) so

infantile I'm sure she could not hear me
listen take in give back one kindly thing

except the ordeal of her inability
to love or be loved therefore hats therefore

she rarely wore a hat I say therefore
because therefore is the most meaningless

word in English it's like cheap pinkish gauze
knowledge of death is what makes this Jew pause

death the haiku koan death the white-winged enemy
friend because I cannot understand why we

were her and me who we were where we were
oh well so much for luck the subject is

love her life of hats may be the one clue
I need to find out why I am the way I

am was will be who I am today clouds
appeared fluffy white above every rooftop

shingled tarred coated with little stones they
looked as solid as a brick wall but you

could not find the cloud you were looking at
when you turned away then looked back change is

what they are their ephemeral splendor
a miracle of acceptance 60

degrees late-March the attack on Iraq
in full swing cameras stationed in Baghdad

sending eerie greenish freeze-motion what
look like underwater shots of the city

to me in America slouched in front
of the TV drinking Scotch now and then

flashes on the horizon red tracers
grenades sirens and shots of tanks striding

the desert refueling men here and there
standing casually in full regalia

unjustly young innocent unopposed
war still at a distance their heavy gear

flickering shadowy sand under their feet
young enough not to fear or fear and not

care if only I could say what freedom is
the person's voice in a poem must be

stripped of itself so as not to reflect
the ego's need to love itself or be

loved the tone might be a stammering
on the threshold a respect for the threshold

because there the silence is the honest
not-knowing of being faced with one's life

if you think autobiographical details
are important I may be able to

dredge up some the gentleness of silence
and the calm it can bring if embraced

is another way atheistic kept here
only by the body whose hands write this

a great man is dying in Princeton I
love him and cannot help he has always

more than anyone I know thought of others
before himself now the dismantlement

of Parkinson's and my sad need to cut
myself off from the pain of loss Ted Weiss

is the name of my friend who is dying
who I have not loved well enough wanted

to spare myself the grief of losing him
strange how the last time I saw him a few

months ago this brilliant man drooled and was
not ashamed offering the example

of his crucifixion grateful to be
with friends I can do nothing the clouds

are still mindlessly reforming themselves
as we must after death according to The Law

and boredom—Life friends is boring we must
not say so—discipline I hear is one key

my answer would be Whatever you do
enjoy it despicable friend *mon frere*

inability to love one's meanest trait
I tried though like Baudelaire with cigar

shot by Charles Neyt 1864 slight scowl
white handkerchief puffed out of left breast pocket

massive brow long strong right hand holding cigar
between index and middle finger hair

cut long in a kind of graying page boy
he tries to see you with his rabid eyes

whether you're there or not the dense black void
of his jacket stuns you with its blackness

the way a baby offers its fresh drek
but you can't look back at him because he

doesn't see you yet in the Carjat photo
1860 a friendly worn-out poet

dressed in a handmade coat vulnerable to
your ever-absent face believes you're there

generous rich gray silk bow-tie large tied loose
right index finger cuticle bitten

pointing down seeks you seems to see you you
whoever you are the someone he you

needs the inner one who is the outer one
you love who loves you better than yourself

his nearly yes piggish noble nose
dominating a broad impassive face

shocking how alive he seems staring in-
to each lens that focuses the light he is

2.

Seedy CB eyes half-closed posed on a
Louis XIII armchair photo signed *Nadar*

in upper left-hand corner I always
wanted to be normal and am like everyone

I know who works pays his bills dozes off dreams
of love but the supreme gift is contradiction

to live in it to *be* it and "People
need not be glued together when they

belong together" makes me cry when you
think of Baudelaire and Whitman 1855

it's amazing the difference in their styles
but both their visions exhort freedom

the American free to be his all-me-you self
the Frenchman a prisoner of self-disgust

pride the desire for "glory" a perverse
"I'm constitutionally sick, and was born

with an execrable temperament because
of my ill-matched parents....That's what comes

of being the child of a twenty-seven-
year-old mother and a sixty-two-year-

old father!" to be a dog is what he
wanted and became a kind of human

dog special mixed breed as yet uncate-
gorized something like mutt fused with whippet

"What will be is. Is is." sang the genius
bitter heartbroken Irish tenor who

takes us where we can only hope cry out
but back to the untellable story

will the truth destroy me some people ask
and death what about death the no life–death

idea of the Zen Buddhists shed body
and mind but how tell me how maybe if

I chose one hat from her stacks in one closet
and put it on and studied my poor head in

the mirror concentrating on the meaning
of the hat on a human head I could

answer the death question its bleak zero
the mere disappearance of someone who

wasn't important to anyone except
himself no matter what they say they know

deep down that if you hadn't existed
they would have done just as well

artists lovers of humanity who
present themselves as good right tender just

need to see themselves that way how many
have the guts to base community on

describing themselves as they really are
"truth stripped of its cloak of time" Conrad said

or Greene's "It seemed after all that one never
really missed a thing" the erotic hair odor

"...they were seldom proud of the invisible"
Greene meditating on women the hat

"...epitomizes the head...so the hat
as a sort of primary idea covers

the whole personality and imparts
its own significance to it. Coronation

endows the ruler with the divine
nature of the sun, the doctor's hood

bestows the dignity of a scholar
and a stranger's hat imparts a strange person-

ality." I always feel that women
look silly in hats men however seem

to wear hats as a natural extension
of the head perhaps because the only

hats I've completely admired have been men's felt Borsalinos
snap brim pork pie especially Lester

Young's tilted up in front just a little
his big baggy eyes sorrowing beneath

oh and hand-woven Irish tweed Jeff Marks
adored to distract people from his huge

hook nose receding chin thin hair narrow
face and skull crowned in cozy wooliness

his small weak eyes saddest I've ever seen
turned down in perpetual sobbing grief

as if to hide the mind or any idea of mind
even the meaning of the word dissolves *mind*

when a hat is on a head the Panamas
(actually made in Ecuador) bone-white the most

intense anti–idea the best Montecristi
finos made in the town of Montecristi

today only twenty weavers left "ob-
viously these are more than hats" the ad

claims Napolean Edward VII George V
of England Roosevelt Heston Gable

the list is fucking endless Twain Wolfe Hoover
the fireman's hat that's the head of a dick

my darling brainless "when the prick goes up
the brains dive into the earth" but the noodle

the squash cannot be understood after
my mother died I found an old photo

of her father as a boy erect holding
the handlebars of his two-wheeler wearing

woolen knickers long black stockings dark jacket
a buttonhole in both lapels white

shirt no tie peak-cap pushed back like a
a bright sepia halo above his teenage face

church walls big chiseled stone blocks behind him
iron spike fence on his left balloon tires

he looks alive though frozen even his
thick black wavy hair flowing out from

under the peak has a poignant lustre
fat shiny bell you ring by pressing

a lever with your thumb in the lower right hand
cardboard corner the pavement is gnawed away

and on the back of the thin mounting board
my mother's hand in blue ink "Father & Bike"

a very subtle koan as I see it
because all of it was real and still is

causing one to feel a dimension of time
outside past present future a psychic

wire stretched between the eyes of the boy looking
straight at anyone who happens to be

there and the eyes of the one who looks back
I think time and identity are threads

intertwined in a way we cannot grasp
identical inseparable and yet

I have no idea why I say that Goodbye
Grandpa are you not really there are you?

such calm cool eyes coatsleeves too short for you
three or four inches of the front forktips

painted white the heavy chain the one-speed sprocket
spokes rims ready to speed away somewhere

how I wish we could talk with each other
people in separate worlds woven together

3.

Do Jews wear hats more of the time than
Gentiles the human noggin hatless deprives

the face of dominating others' faces of
madness and grief face of hello of cash face

of smiling at a friend face thinking of how
it looks to another sick face danger

face utterly incomprehensible
sentient face our own face always unseen

by each of us yet some see only them–
selves when they look at others an infinite

arcane puzzle horrible nameless twisted
in upon itself more viciously

than any other Unattainable
as light from the sun or a new flower

not seeing itself be seen not seeing
self-image in the way finding a hat

that fits looks good isn't easy it's not
the size alone but the feel of the hatband

not too stiff snug or loose hugging the skull
just enough to stay put on a windy day

but still feel as if no hat sat on your head
so hatless you forget you have a hat on

until someone you know stops to chat
and exclaims "God, what a gorgeous hat!"

and makes you take it off so he can look
at the stamped gold words inside the crown study

the feather if there is one each detail
from stitching to texture to whatever

but it's the fit that makes all the difference
when there were gods or God everything

seemed to fit like being a life-long child
protected the way a hat defends a head

against rain snow hail birds disguises just
enough of oneself to bestow the gift

of anonymity on self-consciousness
try it and see a hat above a face

hiding at least one third of the skull
hypnotizes the wearer consoles him

Baudelaire listed the titles of 112
poems and prose poems he planned to write

in these categories *Parisian Topics*
Dream Worlds Symbols and Moralities

Find other categories poem titles
like The Black Hen Flight of Riders

The End of The World I hear Vallejo
singing somewhere in the other world

the poems he wrote still echoing blows in life
more murderous than the hand of God

"Each ribbon of fire seeking love darts quivers
in pitiful roses gives birth to the

burial of the day before—I don't know
if the drumroll where I look for it

will be in clutching a rock or the endless
birth of the heart A grave plumb-line stretches

in hypersensitive axis toward the depth
of beings—Destiny's thread! love will deflect

that law of life toward the voice of man
we'll be free in blue transubstantiation

we'll be virtuous against the blind and fatal
Within every pure zero isolated

in fragile dawns may the superior Jesus
from another great Beginning throb!"

And then one more line—"a Baptist who
watches watches and rides an intangible

curve with one foot bathed in purple" we should
have these words of César printed in-

side every hat from now on so it enters
the mind by osmosis creating a new

holy text a new source matrix for prayer
hats as carriers of texts the words so

close to the brain cells they are soaked up
not memorized penetrate tissue skin bone

take up residence in the soul like a
benign virus whose purpose is to sing

not kill establish a Vallejo Hat
Factory every hat inside bearing

one of his poems but only one kind
of hat is made by the factory a black

fedora (low soft fur felt hat with the crown
creased lengthwise) his autograph stamped there

into the felt one of his lines selected to be
on the leather hatband in big white letters

riding a train plane you could remove
your Vallejo hat look inside it read

his poetry to yourself Pain grows in the world
"Considering coldly that man is sad

that a man stops at times and thinks wanting
to weep his famished mass formula

I love him and affectionately hate him
I make a sign with my hand he comes I hold him close"

don't worry we'll sell to Gentiles *and* Jews
anyone will be able to buy our hats

4.

Number 96 in CB's list of
projected prose poems is called *Death*

whose ever-present leer forms the background
of *Footnotes to an Unfinished Poem* parts

of which were not included in the actual book
an alternate Part 3 for example

recently surfaced published in a small
Irish scholarly journal called SOUL whose

editors felt it was a unique attempt
to define soul's structure in the light of

a couple's doomed obsessive sexual
antics or whatever the right word is

for it and asked the author if any
of the text had been left out so here

is Part 3 which the author did leave out
and let them print: "*1*. Impossible to tell.

Reference to Eternal time as the moment
food enters one's mouth (see Simone Weil on

what she calls the tragedy of sepa-
ration between eyes and mouth in childhood).

Or why Feynman's "In reality, a piece
of glass is a terrible monster of

complexity…" troubled him so deeply.
The one mirror reference in the poem

suggests this metaphysical sense of identity.
No fear of death. *2.* From Aristotle's

De Anima "For the soul is, so to speak,
the first principle of living things." How

the fuck did he know? or as my mother
would say whenever I told her something

I thought would interest her: "Who said so?" And yet
the couple in the poem believed the Greek.

3. Essence of Zen: collapse. "Why seek for a glue
to hold things together when their very

falling apart is the only glue you need?"
(—On Some Hegelisms, W. James)

"…irreducible the contingencies
of the world." (Ibid) They failed to heed either

but realized the truth of Wordsworth's
"I've watched you now a full half hour/Self-

poised upon that yellow flower" where
according to WW complete attention

shrinks time into a blessed eternal
instant. Poontang as Baptist version of

Zen. Guitar chord. No taste. *4.* "In the wilderness
of Great Mind no one gets lost." (Notebooks of

SB) Reference in this couplet to blueprints
of a machine that would do it for you.

Small enough to store on a shelf or carry
in purse or briefcase. Vibration range

very broad according to sexual need.
5. Devastating sense of the feeble power

of words. "How often we would sit there trying
to say…" This line and the following three

define the "language-limit" theme. Reference
is to Blanchot's "The unknown is always

thought in the neuter," from *The Infinite
Conversation*. 6. From Dogen's "Uji"

(Being-Time). "Nevertheless, doubting
itself, for the time being, is indeed

time." Such pseudo-profundities (?) and their
infuriating promise form the very

core of the poem's intention to exhaust
erotic possibility and break through

into some…"Kingdom of Unity"? 7.
Clit-tonguing as wisdom. Yum-yum-yum.

"Intended meaning is a donkey, ex-
pression is a horse." They slept through this.

8. In this position they sense the final
barrier. Sudden recall of one of the

greatest haiku ever penned, Bang-foo's

blue cloudless sky's
four-foot long rhino cock's
a worldless book

9. "It is necessary then that they smell
without breathing in…" (II. 9 *De Anima*,

on sound and hearing) "And it will also
be clear why fish are without voice…" This

fucker doesn't miss a trick! Application
general. 10. "…no fury like a Christian stoned,/

nothing but the blank pupils of his eyes."
These surreal revisions and juxtapositions

attempt to express the theme of redemption
through loss, but it obviously fails

to do so. Who is the thrower, who
the stoned? 11. American poet:

jocose reference here to his money his
viciousness stinginess sexual

incompetence arrogance faked compassion
whose books earned him the title of "village

explainer." The silence of a full mouth
made speech impossible for her, all she

could do was nod, bobbing up and down on it.
12. This moment between them was as if

light and time actually did become one
in the misguided mirrors of their faces

facing each other. Pure pathe. Sword. Wound.
"Because I can polish glass." Newton's answer

to a question about "…the deep mystery
of partial reflection." (QED) *13.* "Thus

light is something like raindrops…" Feynman's poeti-
cism in QED inspires, consoles them,

but not for long. "As silent as a mirror
is believed…" Hart Crane's neologistic

analogy is nearly what it points to,
and will not go away. *14.* The wish

to solve a problem always means that the
problem will outlive the limitations

of language. Kneeling is the only
solution. Like a dog begging for scraps.

Like a penitent. Like a gardener.
Like a cocksucker. It doesn't matter.

That is the only valid position.
Their discipleship. *15.* "Is counter-love,

original response./But what he cried…"
Frost's great gloss in "The Most of It" on their

plight. *16.* "Originally writing was
the voice of an absent person." (Freud). One

of those countless amazing asides from
the great mind-tamer's revelatory pen. One

might connect S. Weil's "The World, inasmuch
as it is entirely empty of God,

is God himself. And the abandonment
in which God leaves us is his own way

of caressing us," to the word "person"
in Freud's little theory. Hard for them

to resist such inflated interpretations
of ordinary words. *17.* Their

pathetic attempts at scientific
explanations of why they are doomed. Mice

gnawing the sugar-coated bars of their cage.
18. This section of the poem entirely

without landscape, as if the human
needed nothing but itself. Empty space

a reference to their inexhaustible
lust to transcend. Are we all like that? Cf.

Parmenides of Elea's "I wept
and wailed when I saw the unfamiliar

land (at birth)." *19.* Surely they would have
found rest if they could have understood, used

in their situation, Anaximander's
deep "Nozzle of the bellows." *20.* "For

it is not every sound of an animal
that is a voice…rather it is necessary

that that which strikes be ensouled and have a
kind of imagination, as voice as voice is

a kind of sound with meaning and not,
like a cough…" Aristotle again. Wow!

21. "Unless it was the embodiment
that crashed"—line following the two quoted

above (15.) says it all. Also captured
in Frost's forgotten poem "Escapist—Never,"

another unexpected, disregarded
paradigm of our couple's insoluble

(universal?) dilemma. 22. Critias
of Athens (flourished about 475 BC):

"Purchase of fish. To buy fish. To watch
the price of fish." This became their chant

or anthem to spur them on whenever
they fell back. Also used as a mantra

for insomnia. 23. "There is no reason,
as it seems to me, why the emotional

factor of conviction should enter into
this question at all." (SF in Beyond

The Pleasure Principle) Another
definition of free choice. But our

characters are far from The Promised Land.
Kafka's "I feel restless and vicious" is

easily misunderstood as a complaint
instead of the prelude to revelation

it is in the unfinished poem (HERE) behind these
footnotes. Not quoted in the poem, but

its dark surgery is implied. "Where was I
who was I trying to be while being me?"

5.

Hats. Almost forgot hats. Those two astounding closets.
Protect the head. My mother covered hers.

Finally, around March 15 (1866)
Baudelaire left for Namur where he stayed

with the Rops family. During his visit
to the Eglise Saint-Loup he collapsed on

the flagstones; suffering from a cerebral
disorder, was taken back immediately

to Brussels. "…that poetry must be un-
related to morality but not opposed."

5,000 francs in debt. 1865.
2,000 paid off he's back in Paris

for 5 days, can't afford a train ticket.
In the station Mendes suddenly found

himself face to face with Baudelaire
"I saw the wretched state of his clothes—

perfectly proper, no doubt, but worn
and shiny in places—and, with his unshaven

face, he looked almost menacingly sullen,
the way he did on the day the bills came due…

he would certainly have preferred not to
run into anyone. I was about

to apologize and go away, when he
turned pleasant and affectionate, and took

me by the arm. We left the station
together. He explained that he had come

to Paris on business, that he was going back
to Brussels, that he had missed the evening

train, and would spend the night in a hotel,
leaving the next day on the first train."

Mendes lived close to the station in the
rue de Douai and offered to share his rooms.

"Do you know, my boy, how much money I've
earned since I've been working, since I've been alive?"

Anguished bitter sour reproach protest
in his voice the men facing each other

"I shall count it up for you! (Along
with the amounts he had received for them

he reeled off lists of his articles, verse
poems, prose poems, etc. added them

all up in his head suddenly proclaimed
"Total profit from all my life: fifteen

thousand, eight hundred and ninety-two francs,
sixty centimes!" He burst out laughing then

extinguished the lamp "Now," he said, "let us
sleep." ("I sometimes receive, from very distant

places, and from people whom I do not
know, tokens of sympathy which touch me

deeply, but which do not console me
for my loathsome poverty, my

humiliating situation, nor
especially for my vices.")

"Must I tell you—you who realized no more
than anyone else—that in that *horrific*

book, I put all my *heart*, all my *tenderness*,
all my *religion* (disguised), all my *hate*?"

kissed by the exquisite lips of Syphilis
now all day all night in Brussels where they

splash water over the pavements in large
buckets every morning damp soil bad food

& no one knows what his disease is I
too am diseased "Your mother injected

her insanity into you" you'll recall
she had as much lovelight in her body

held against mine so much lightless light
wrapped up in the silent crow of his mind

or the times she would not give me money
to eat and purchased hats instead and lectured

me on the importance of glass hats glass
feathers and hatbands raw brims that the light

could flow through so he and I in very
serious condition no matter what

the differences even though he went out
for a walk with his head wrapped in a kerchief

and a dull pain over the right eyebrow
it would be helpful to the reader if

a theory emerged from all this in order
to write he was forced to plaster a compress

on his forehead soaked every hour in
sedative water and take tablets with

opium valerian digitalis balladona
in them dizziness vomiting falling

head first "and I haven't a penny!"
hallucinations of his mother's eyes

staring at him while he dozed or wrote
letters "One evening, without having drunk

or eaten anything, I started rolling
over like a drunkard, grabbing pieces

of furniture, pulling them over with me.
Vomiting bile or white froth. These are

invariably the different stages:
I'm perfectly well, and haven't eaten,

and then all at once, without warning,
for no apparent reason, I feel haziness,

distraction, stupor, followed by terrible
pain in the head. Really all I can do

is fall over unless I'm lying
on my back when it happens. Then cold sweat,

vomiting and protracted stupor. The illness
persists and the doctor pronounced the great word

hysteria, which means I'm raving mad.
He wants me to do lots and lots of walking.

For the first time I've given into
the desire to feel sorry for myself.

Do you know this sort of illness? Have you
ever seen anything remotely like it?

What's really *ridiculous* is that a man
walking behind me, or a child or dog

going past make me feel like fainting.
The only sensible thing the doctor told me

(in my opinion) was 'Take cold baths
and go swimming' but in the damned city

there's no river. It's true they've invented
swimming pools or artificial ponds in which

the water is heated a little by
a nearby machine. It's horrible

just to think about it. I have no
desire to bathe in an artificial

lake polluted by all those filthy pigs."
Sometimes I'm sure you've felt it too anywhere

out of this world I'd give anything to be
somewhere else not not here exactly here

but only if some metaphysical
approximation could be added to it

"Again, some things exist and come into
being of which there are no Forms..." some

idea of self that makes one feel being here
is exactly as it should be like grass-

or cloud-consciousness not conscious of self
but purely itself without the evil ill-

ness of culture physical neither in-
side themselves nor outside the way hats

have neither an inside nor an outside
as Jesus said about cups "Why

do you wash the inside of the cup?
Did not He who made the inside also

make the outside?" The hat that Conrad had
his ship captain drop on the ominous unknown

waters a mystic marker a buoy
to negotiate the shoreline so he

can leave the secret sharer there a killer
the captain split himself yet not himself

in the terror of his first voyage hat–
less letting the hat think for him letting

his own identity be healed by the stranger
a headless hat floating in moonlight

alongside the hull the famed crown of thorns
nothing but consciousness itself *the* hat

of hats who was more out of this world than
Jesus? faith like alcohol drunk on faith

testicular was the first word Baudelaire
dreamed in remission in 1866

hallucinating for a split-second
Christ's balls hung naked where the loincloth was

the pubic hair not sparse but densely
bunched penis semi-erect while the still

breathing man–God's wordless torment swathed
his mind or perhaps *gonad* whatever

the word is it began a new poem he
could never finish The Naked Christ Sonnet

"I would prefer a softer hat than this spiked thing
even a beret would be better than these green leaves

punctuating my brow with thorns torturing me
and both my testicles cry out my penis grieves

and not one person witnessing this will help me down
or warm my genitals with their lips I see

the face of God descending like the shattered wing
of some unnameable bird from nowhere nothing

comes from its mouth not one soothing word
from the face tells me why I am up here"

the unfinished poem ends scribbled out
in bed the poet dreaming about Paris

17 months from death meanwhile he would
continue struggling with his testicle

poem and the ever-recurring hat
fiasco that consumed him that he thought

would be his greatest poem by far even
Anywhere Out of the World XLVIII

in *Paris Spleen* could not rival it though
that prose poem rubs our noses in its

theme of mankind's perpetual demand
to be elsewhere and his plan to write

The Great Prayer and *Death* he did begin *Death*
which was to be a new definition

of The Beyond "Which one of us can see
the Other Side where no one is himself

where otherness is what each person is
and no one has a name and no one fears

nothing but sky and voices crisscrossing
like a billion choirs singing one necessary song?

How wordlessly they sing how the sweet air
of heaven and the stupid fires of hell

punish the minds of those who are alive
and think their speech has meaning think they know

who is who isn't what is here and where
what isn't is cold screwdriver ideas

hats of lust betrayal broken tongues
mumbling the nonsense of ten thousand years"

contrary to the doctors' advice and the pleas
of his friends he continued to use and abuse

stimulants fragments of *The Great Prayer*
did get written "as if torn by desire"

"the hairy sac in which they swing swelling
with venom" "her gonad-hungry tongue"

"God gave us what we" "the poor have eyes like
old translucent grapes" "forgiveness isn't"

but *he* never realized the poem just left
ragged notes fragments sketching his decision

to praise God blame God exonerate God
whose existence he doubted but believed in

anyhow these are only rough translations
of his exquisite French old battered hats

6.

"I am neither well nor sick. I work and
write with difficulty," he wrote to his mother

after a mild stroke. "The face is still
intelligent, and thoughts seem to pass over it

in a flash. I think he experiences
some pleasure when he hears a friend's name.

Despite my recommendations Baudelaire
has been placed in a clinic run by un-

supervised nuns. So far Baudelaire has
refused to give them the satisfaction

of even the most elementary signs of faith."
At this point who can forget the poet's

"There are days when I feel so powerful that…"
recorded in a letter years earlier

probably at about the time he wrote
Anywhere Out of the World—"This life

is a hospital each patient in it
tortured by the longing to occupy

a different bed one wants to suffer near
the stove one believes if he could stretch out

next to the window he'd be healed I know
I'd always feel good somewhere else I'm always

arguing with my soul about somewhere else
soul my poor chilled soul what about Lisbon

it's warm there you'd be calm self-confident
like a lizard the city's on the water

built of marble soul the citizens hate
the vegetable kingdom so furiously

they uproot all the trees you'd like that landscape
landscape of light and minerals water

to reflect them my soul says nothing back
since you like rest so much linked with the spectacle

of movement why not live in Holland country
of bliss you'd probably love it there

theme of so many paintings what about
Rotterdam you love a wilderness of masts

ships moored at the foot of houses my soul
silent Batavia might be better

European plus tropical beauty
not one word from you my soul are you dead

or so numb only pain is pleasureable
if so let's live only where the death's head's

embroidered on the national flag Torneo
far edge of the Baltic or beyond to the Pole

where sunlight glances off the earth light moves
so slowly night and day are almost the same

there's no variety it's all monotony
that other face of the void there we'll take

long baths of darkness while the Northern Lights
send us their pink bouquets when they care to

like a fireworks show in hell exploding
inside your face in a glass you stare into

at last I hear you and your wise advice
anywhere! anywhere out of the world!"

7.

If the subject of death isn't dealt with properly
one might mistake life for death death for life

I mean that since they are two sides of the same
piece of paper how are we supposed to

read the texts of our lives is one side blank
and the other a mess of heavy scrawls

even in the passion of traffic fervid
notes ball-pointed onto the paper while

we eat lunch or dodge a crazy driver
bent on running me down crossing on the green

the fact that I have lived in a cage all
my life should not stop you from listening

others have sung others have tried to write
public truth under personal conditions

as limited as mine inside a house
or teaching talking about golf to Keith

Philly's most conscious bartender now near
divorce with a new daughter Emily

one life ends another is not begun
a man can't live between two worlds forever

never fully exist or exist more no excuses
no blame each person in a life stationed

exactly where he is not necessarily
good for anyone else much as we try

often in the middle of the night
I wake thinking of people I have not

loved or have hurt or used or treated as if
they mattered only to others disdained

do we really want to know each other
intimately or is it merely lone

yearning searching for touch for words O *you*
trace of . . . and death we say to ourselves

can save us from what for what the fact is
life is detail dictating every act

us the world the world us invisibly
married to each other every step of the way

and Baudelaire is dying in a book
I'm reading he eats he sleeps he goes out

in a carriage or on foot with a walking-stick
with friends can't read furious can't speak

his mother arrives puts up at the Grand Miroir
burning to treat him "like a little child"

8.

It's their caps and hats held out like cups
to receive coins that make the poor so

despicable their filthy insides reeking
of grime and hair their emptiness like consciousness

sick with the irremediable need
for happiness "I can't stand those people

with their eyes as wide open as coal bunkers!"
the poet shouts in one of his prose poems

about society in another he beats up
a beggar who dangles his cap knocks two

teeth out tries to strangle him bashes
his head against a wall seizes a thick branch

lying on the ground then pounds him like a cook
trying to soften a 10-year-old steak

the man leaps up punches Baudelaire
in the eye knocks out four teeth thanks him

no memory of sound left no memory
and a dirty hairbrush thrown across the room

and a dirty hat brushed off we walked
through the fields his joy at being alive

his happiness his eyes raised up to heaven
speechlessly then back to Paris "When I

saw him walking toward me supported by
M. Stevens, leaning on his left arm, with

his walking stick tied to his coat-button,
I wept, he saw me and laughed a resonant

long drawn-out laugh which made my blood run cold.
The part of him that the illness had spared

was perfectly fit and active, his mind
was as free and nimble as the year before."

March 31, 1867 unable to move
watched over by his mother "Look here, how

can you possibly believe in God?" B.
pointed to the sky clouds aflame gold fire

"*Crenom! oh! Crenom!*" he yelled in protest
trying to bring down the sky with his fist

9.

In one of his trunks jammed full of papers
opened after his death parts of the hat

poem were written out in deep blue ink on
18 sheets of paper some with only

a few sentences lists of phrases
others crowded from edge to edge lines

stacked on top of each other nearly touching
one page had a loony footnote he meant

to be one key to the hat poem's meaning
its emotional and religious core

a justification of the object
that had been invented to sit on top

of a human head designed redesigned
endlessly until it came to stand for

some vision of the pure true clear godhead
or source "For there is analogy between

all the categories of being—
as 'straight' is in length, so is 'level' in

breadth, perhaps 'odd' in number and 'white'
in color." but the footnote to the hat

poem its validity as a tool
of interpretation is what needs

to be understood here is the footnote—
"Gamete, from Greek *gametes* husband, from

gamein to marry: a mature male or
female germ cell usually possessing

a haploid chromosome set and capable
of initiating formation of a new

diploid individual by fusion
with a gamete of the opposite sex"

a lesser key may be the sentence
"For each hat, because of its character,

evokes a face and lets the mind's eye see it."
probably the most fabulous idea

about hats ever expressed followed by
"Guillotined heads." (quoted much earlier)

the poem inscribed in bold slanted letters
on genuine vellum has no order

no beginning or end a reader
because the pages are not numbered

has to collate organize edit intuit
who knows what word applies to the manuscript

and is therefore in a sense one of the
authors of the poem if it is a poem

not merely a random epitaph of
language-pointers for example I

might begin the poem with the phrases
"Death as executioner. Death as friend."

which appear side by side on one of those pages
or "A clean task." disconnected alone

among such others as "Where then can one
find a cup deep enough and a dagger

thick enough to drown the *Beast*!"
these seem to be like speech reaching out as

real hands defining the devastated.
islands of the soul uninhabited

inaudible torments joys "I live
forever in a building on the point

of collapsing, a building undermined
by a secret malady." the beauty

of that the imperishable truth or
"I can no longer find the way out."

but why a song of loss about hats why
sadness of hats funeral of hats death-stained hats

Baudelaire seems to have known a good deal
about Japanese poetry which may explain

the apparent esthetic randomness
the calligraphic jabs and streaks and white

spaces like the 4% of light bouncing
off glass marble to pass through it a diploid

phenomenon? the hat poem tries to
pinpoint that area where the actual hat

that hides the top of the head delineates
its place in the history of ideas

how the touch of skull against cotton straw
establishes a vital connection

between the bone that shields the mind and what
might penetrate and poison intellect

"If I were king I'd crown each human head
with a gold halo…" is one fragment of

the equality of all things "The self
is described as *not this, not that*" says

the Brihadaranyaka Upanishad hats
too are neither one nor the other

the packet of unnumbered pages quotes
"Anything that is not the Self perishes"

not this not that means that to wear a hat
or to walk out with a naked head are

the same but the object "of a felt hat
hand made raw edge putty-colored pinched

in front by a loving hand just so"
is a supreme example of religious faith

because of the way light lies tentatively among
the folds along the elegant skin-like

surfaces of the hat no question I
have never seen two hats exactly

alike a revelation that imparts
equanimity to this ruined man

at the end of his baffling life
but it grows clearer and clearer that most

people although they may own several
hats rarely wear them unless it rains

snows or the sun is so intense they fear
heatstroke or wake up in a jolly mood

and want to celebrate by wearing a hat
that has nothing to do with anything

except showing off this head in that hat
and fuck you if you think it looks silly

I remember my mother used to put
a woolen hat she knitted on my head

in winter pull it down over my ears
before she let me go out sledding she

liked hats on my head all kinds baseball caps
beanies I had one with a plastic propeller

on top my father always had fancy
gray and brown felt hats brims trimmed in silk

feathers in the bands creased on top believed
they would make him look more "professional"

why hats came to be will always elude
the paleontologist of head ornaments

why anyone would care is also one
of those questions people ask who have lost

their sense of how amazing is
an authentic sombrero ten gallon

why ask at all hats are as we are in-
explicable though we seem indispensable

to ourselves but hats too have a life simple
as it is otherwise why would they be

everywhere hanging on hooks in stores
piled up on racks advertised in The New Yorker

not why but which one on what occasion
opera ballgame trout fishing business lunch

why this is an elegy I can see now
obviously hats wait longer than other clothes

to be worn compared to shoes eyeglasses
underpants socks shirts belts trousers so

in my mother's closets and in my own
I can hear hats weeping for themselves

whispering *useless useless* to each other
one or two fallen to the floor others

lost out of style crushed unseasonal it's
tragic the way hats essential as they are

continue to be treated as outcasts
just as the unquotable impossible-

to-arrange posthumous shattered elegy
on hats by *mon semblable* must

always remain unknown like the sky he
tried to punch a hole through to touch God

10.

Without the letters my grandfather born
in Paris willed me as his legacy

how could any scholar know about
that suave skullcap that black lustrous serious

beanie white too *yarmulkah* (originally
Turkish for "rainwear") Baudelaire owned

wore several he stole from various
synagogues I only know that he was

Jewish secretly converted attended
services often even when stoned on

hashish pussy brandy his hunger for
belief so intense so pointlessly

without objective substantiation
like all of us victimized by the pain

of the absence of love the pain of God's
invisibility whatever Simone

thought proved God exists a mystic's love
battered his heart true mystics open their souls

to the oncoming wave sure of themselves
because they feel within something realer

than themselves they prove to be great men
of action to the surprise of those

for whom mysticism is nothing but visions
raptures ecstasies that which they have let

flow into them is a stream rushing
down seeking through them to reach their

fellow-men the necessity to give
to others what they have received affects

them like an onslaught of love a love
each one of them expresses in his own code

personality a love which in each of them
is an entirely new inscape capable

of transposing human life into another tone
a love which thus causes each of them to be

loved for himself so that through him
and for him other men will open

their souls to the love of humanity
is there a mystic dormant in each of us

simply waiting for an occasion to awake
skullcap so light upon the head we forget

it's there "Here not here nowhere to rest no
life lightless I burn myself away soul

free of me soars whispering only to God
therefore I suffer infinitely my

grief is slight even without myself
heaven is here Love fuels my life my black

blind day grace works invisibly I've learned
I don't know how and all my good & evil

tastes like a lover's mouth soul given unto
itself swallowed in sweet fire I quench

instantly the least light burn myself away"
so St. John of the Cross sang his dark night

but such delicate weight the touchless touch
of the yarmulkah is the transient breath

of a faceless atheist Baudelaire wrote
in his diary "I always wore one in private."

had several made some with a button on top
some perfectly smooth mohair linen merino

having memorized portions of Vedic
texts he would often chant phrases to excite

himself convinced that the erect penis
is an omen of holy significance

the harder and longer held the more untainted
more virulent what future event though

beyond the sensitive throbbing tip's hunger
is impossible to say but that nightstick's

irresistible force was enough to shake
the skullcap from his head he had a cedar

box made (he noted) to keep them smelling fresh
over a hundred piled up packed close

so unassumingly delicate small harmless
rich as the iris of a finch's eye

or the blood of Christ at dusk on the cross
this odd thing is true too he would often

wear a yarmulkah under other hats
it was so easy to do in order

to remind himself (and God) that he was a Jew
heretic devout Hebrew poet who

wanted above all to convert sin
by alchemical means into the goodness

of love that sees all things as equal all
people as each other and themselves

"Pain is the recognition by the living
creature that its body is being deprived

of the image of the soul." who can say
what it is in his *Journaux intimes* his

overwhelming thirst to make room for
a living icon of the human spirit that

bypasses the pious dome of the yarmulkah
with "To screw is to aspire to enter

into another person, and the artist
never goes outside himself." "Only the brute

has no trouble getting a hard-on, and
screwing is the lyricism of the masses."

"Love is the desire to prostitute oneself."
"The most prostituted being is the Supreme

Being, God Himself, since for every
individual he is the friend

above all others, since he is the common
inexhaustible reservoir of love."

"…that ineffable orgy, that holy
prostitution of the soul which, in an

act of poetry and charity, gives itself
entirely to the unexpected and to

the unknown…a holy and degrading
openness." it was only when wearing

the tender nebish hand-of-God skullcap
that the poet felt free to dig for truth

without shame or fear of public reproach
some nights he would sleep with a few of them

stacked on his head even lay one over
his face believing it was his mother's hand

barely weighing on his eyelids "Of the
vaporization and centralization

of the Ego. Everything depends on that."
"There is, in prayer, a magical operation…

And what is not a prayer? To shit is prayer…"
"God is a scandal—a scandal which pays."

under those flimsy umbrellas his brain
would fulfill its religious aims to crush

all values into their opposites a powder
of contradiction resembling dandruff

under the cap designed to soothe the mind
with its near absence weightless wisp of soul

to plunge my hands into a mound of skullcaps
to feel their epidermal rose petal surfaces

caress my hands to hold them there breathlessly
until the chilly fabrics feel like my own skin

would be like hearing God mumble my name
with no intention but to let me know

He is conscious of my existence in
his uncaring trust one of Baudelaire's rages

caused him to destroy the yarmulkahs
by tossing those petite bonnets into his fireplace

one by one he aimed them at the logs
watching them flare up in single brief red

puffs their ashes mixed indistinguish-
shably with woodash not one pathetic skullcap

left sheer figments now one especially
sewn by a child yellow six-pointed star

embroidered brightly on top to stare back
at stars massed in the inhuman firmament

each fixed in its arbitrary space bluewhite
as a baby's eye seeing what it sees

and smashed the empty box with his bootheel
and threw handfuls of splinters on the low fire

11.

Every funeral I've been to (Jewish of course)
had a table in the lobby piled high

with yarmulkahs I always saved mine
to remind me that death is real *real*

as a girlfriend's adored hairpie so when
I'd go down on her (often as possible,

naturally) I'd say to myself Stevie this is
the death kiss the wet-faced blindly complete

giving oneself back to the beginning
a kind of tongue-tied aria faceless

homage to no God except the moans bird-
sounds drifting out of the far-away mouth

I was delving except the no one I was
that prayer-like state whether on one's knees

or stretched out flat head between those heaven-
ward legs I confess a few times just for fun

in the dark I'd slip one of those idiot
frizbees out of my pants pocket and doff it

as my head slowly descended upon
I suppose what many would call the world's

most sought-after insatiably hot targets
and go to work not as a mere layman

but as a religious fanatic self-made
saint-rabbi performing my daily good deed

with my whole self all the time the black tortilla
on top clinging to my hair probably

because of its sexual electricity
then it would fall off get lost in the sheets

finally every one I promised to save
got lost death reminded me all by itself

more persistently then more than with or
without yarmulkahs it was all too painful

so what big deal Death is a German expert
and all that crap down there with a hard-on

in your lips hair cooze juice up to your eyebrows
what's death an occupation for the saint

Dickinson's vision #1445
Death is the supple suitor/That wins at last—/

It is a stealthy Wooing/Conducted first/
By pallid innuendoes/And dim approach/

But brave at last with Bugles/And a
bisected Coach/It bears away in triumph/

To Troth unknown/And kindred and responsive/
As porcelain. amazing how the faces

of the dead remain precise in the mind
then mind by mind fade thin out disappear

less clear each time until a mind appears
without those named faces roaming it

you can see feel in Baudelaire palpable
death the evicted tenant death the drained

ravaged face overcoat jacket hair pomaded cigar
bowtie furious eyes handkerchief fingers frown

shirt cuff black backdrop against black cloth brow
bursting with the black vomit of fury and death

not that I planned to create this mood now
insoluble impasse the shit koan

famous for its indigestible truth
like a snot-sized knot of wrought iron

if you've ever seen a dog's hind legs stiffen bend
the dog squat concentrated in a trance

eyes glazed or closed you must have noticed
that the feces issuing from its anus—

(often it takes minutes before the first
glimmer of excrement shows itself)

loose or shapely stools—falls in a neat pile
as though it and the animal were one

silent deathsong sung under consciousness
immortality "weakest point in the ego" Hakuin's

"Punch your fist mind of a fist through this black wall
always in front of you always the next step

you can't take as you walk into it through it
but can't because it's who you are but can't be

do not want to be nothing but the place
where you were are won't be slam this fist

of a fist into the wall that isn't
even here built of a billion nows yous

which when it finally is you finally face it
you pass through like a raw black breath"

a badge announcing HERE COMES A JEW! or
a black duncecap (Middle Ages law) now

they vary not only black a Jew is free
to design his own personal skullcap

to express whoever he thinks he is
what he believes how he wants to be known

it separates the human from the sky
it shows humility it covers that

so-called sapient brain that civilizing
meathook of a mentation hanging empty

in an icecold locker stick a hat on it
white satin contraption with a tulle veil

call it history or art a question
for contemporary metaphysics

God's will stigmata faith Freud's big dog Lun
oh None-Of-The-Above may be the name

of the new God we haven't found to worship
if I decide to make my own yarmulkah

I'll use blue faille sew tiny gold lamé six-pointed
stars all over it my own cryptic sky

clapped atop my head and I confess
I'd never take it off even to shower

fuck sleep leave it on in the pouring rain
wear it to parties thrown by the goyim

inside the label reads *Bergida*
original Hungarian one-of-a-kind

Jewboy headpiece in homage to in fear of
the Lord or sunstroke like the word of God

heard thundering across the sky in Margate
right over Castle's deli incredible

chopped liver herring even Gentiles shopped
those aisles that guaranteed stroke heart attack

I had this idea one day picking out bagels
(plain) that you could use one as a vagina

smear the inside of the hole with what?—butter
cream cheese sour cream strawberry jam egg salad?

that's how I often took my mind off God-
lessness our old chaos of the sun unsponsored

free who needs it? "intolerable" Freud called it
"for we who suffer grievously from life"

deer walk upon our mountains and the quail
whistle about us their spontaneous cries

my ass! if I could have a yarmulkah
made out of skin lifted from my thigh

grafted onto the top of my shaved head maybe
that would make His face appear on the gray stone

wall of Meersault's cell and mine not that I
would believe in it or let the priest in that story

kiss me but at least the memory of a glimpse of...
illusory crazed desperate to construct

a flimsy image at least as worthless as
toilet paper flushed by the swirling water

all that's left of our faith in a deity
Baudelaire caught it with his sonnet *Chasm*—

"Pascal's chasm splits me in two, I live it.
The world's an abyss—action, speech, reverie,

lust! Wind crashes through the enormous fear
of my hair crackling with electric fire.

Above, below, everywhere, ocean floor, shore,
silence panics space into ice;

God's wise forefinger can't stop scribbling
in the earth a nightmare of my nights.

Sleep's dim cruddy pit swallows me—
flesh, mud, shit: I'm not sure what or where—

infinity feeds infinity outside my windows. . .
Every instant battered by dizziness,

jealous of numb nothingness, oh my mind, pity me,
I'll never escape Numbers and Creatures!"

itself some kind of wordhat that explains
mind to itself staves off the hatred *nada*

pues nada while the young lovers pass by
under the chestnut trees behind the rich

old man drunk on brandy in the bright café
wrapt in a long sweet kiss under lamplight

they are sure will keep them safe forever
unaware of him who a few weeks ago

tried to hang himself was cut down
by his daughter his forehead on the table

his black beret on the floor "Many must
have it" says the young waiter to himself

sleeplessly I wouldn't let any priest
kiss my ass even if he could produce God's face

12.

Who knows what Baudelaire meant by "The Great
Prayer" staking out the future titles listed

under Parisian Topics Dream Worlds Symbols
& Moralities "I do not tie

the recalcitrant will to the unending
thread of a superfluous plot." but he

must have dreamt of a godless prayer far beyond
the precincts of our failure to have faith

the words of other prayers he knew he
must have begged for a prayer savaged by life

in "In all misfortune there is but one
danger: when the sufferer will not believe

that misfortune is good fortune. This is
perdition…" and Soren's "For what is self-torment?

It is the worry which today (having
enough worry of its own) does not have.

And what is it to be a self-tormentor?
It is to cause oneself this worry, for

the bird also has worry the one day
it lives, the day may have for it too enough

worry of its own; but the worry of
the next day the bird does not have—because

it lives but one day, which we might express
also in another way, by saying

that it has no self. Worry and today
are in correspondence with one another;

self-torment and the next day are also a pair.
But how then is the bird a teacher?

Quite simply. That the bird has no next day
is sure enough—so then, be thou like the bird,

get rid of the next day, and thus thou art
without the anxiety of self-torment;

and this must be practicable, precisely
for the reason that the next day is

derived from the self…Oh of all enemies
which assail a man by might or cunning,

none perhaps is so obstinately in-
trusive as this next day, which is always

the same next day…When a man lives absorbed
in today, he turns his back to the next day."

kind fierce Kierkegaard offers us in his
Christian Discourses I sometimes think

hopeless prayer pointlessly writhing in its
mess of unformed words is the only true prayer

but I'm not sure what CB's Great Prayer would be
the one we'd listen to memorize thank

use need most vision we have waited for
forever like St. Mark's chilling report

"23 And he took the blind man by
the hand, and led him out of the town; and

when he had spit on his eyes, and put
his hands upon them, he asked him if he

saw ought. 24 And he looked up, and said,
I see men as trees, walking. 25 After that

he put *his* hands again upon his eyes,
and made him look up: and he was restored,

and saw every man clearly." *precaria*
feminine of *precarius* to pray

only if it is done not to obtain
anything is it The Great Prayer—I *think*—

should it be a story about how we are
"bereft of our place among the animals"

after my mother died what could I do
with her hats first I had to empty

the two closets pack them into cardboard
liquor store boxes tape them figure out

how to get rid of them I saved a few
I knew friends would like all of them animal

skins mink broadtail nutria sable
leopard raccoon ermine fox rabbit all

from the thoughtless species and one velour
tomato red cloche a single stripe of felt

zigzagging across its right side like black
lightning and one blue twill rainhat each head

takes up just so much room in a given
hat one of the disreputable math problems

what is the average centimeter head depth
in say 1000 hats seated on 1000

human heads take that number and divide
by 3 adopt the dumb trance of the sponge

and you'll be there in the music not the
why or when in the high music wrapped

in indomitable me the number
you get from the division above will

be like telling your misery to the birch
offering your backyard sky to the dumb bird

pecking dirt on the brick patio where
the dust of the story that is you is

the no-view dust of Nagarjuna I
am trying to tell you what is despair

composed of if not the flesh the lonely
skin the blind woman in my dream who loved me

because she could not see me shielded by
her blindness I loved her too she held my face

moved her breasts against me some sound like a
buzzing some soul sighing itself into me

letting the love between us saturate us
her face against my ear her entire body

given unto me lips touching my ear
breath-words note-words self listening self heard

throat genital spirit whispering The Prayer
how can you know what it means to be here

in the clear silence without need listening
fed by the lost source of nature where you

are now voices hover breathe on the abyss
are the abyss bare songs faint streaks traces

gusts scribble of leaves cloud scrawl unpredictable
storms calms black trees tablet of weeds and stars

you could die here watching pink twilit haze
become night daybreak dusk igniting the

dark water step into the flickering
meadow beyond opening to you its

bright deep surface a mind not yours throat
humming before we had our lives places

cry out for images of you of me
if they had tongues what could they say to

explain us what do the crazy years do
to us who hope to live forever sure

of a life after in the tenderness
of knowing this amazed by cherry branches

each blossoming stripped in a day o gods
we hear speaking to us on pages time

fuses its cold flame to our souls we put
our human hands together pray murmur

your names that are no one's this tiny body
of flesh of bone answerless composing

its last message again again again
but the river consoles urgent hypnotic

geese drift on the rough water mirror
holding nothing spilling across falls long

body mouth fireladen sky in it where
all images are broken on the meeting

of two eternities between by white
chrysanthemums scissors hesitate

only an instant no words to say it
thought these rise from anonymous stone to

help the mystery speak like a letter to
an intimate friend and not hinder the

sacred troubled beauty love is was will be
love has shaken me like wind rushing down

from the hills hitting an oak you
burn me with what eyes look me in the face

friend to friend nothing's sweeter than sleeping
with your love it heals the dying soul with

what eyes what pain love gives you burn me show
me what's behind your eyes of death's tremendous

nearness kneeling to any phrase hear me
talking in my sleep to you to whom I

gave birth how can you know what it means how
can you face the edge of time who does not

think of himself is given the keys offerings
glimpses of torn mist who the kindness

infinite of my hands who now where you
stand touch me give me my name

13.

You'd think the mind would just wear itself out
the way a hat does but old hats I love

coverings hats galore Filson Tincloth Polo
black cotton USA Baltimore Oriole

replica it's comforting each day to
pass the coatrack hooks smothered by toppers

and decide which one or whether I will
still it's the rapture intrinsic

to hats to speculate on the darkness
inside waiting to be filled with a head

self-glorification only I/you
knows the meaning of which delineates who you

really are really in the sense of no
image or idea beyond self-knowledge

more like the fragrance of a particular
early morning on a wet Mexican street

or a fact like Montecristo *finos*
must be woven between midnight and 6 a.m.

to protect the straw from damage who will
make those hats after the last 20 weavers

die are they teaching their sons oh old old hats
old hats that finally fit so well they feel

when you put one on that it and your head
belong together married the same

entity no hat without a head no
sine mixtura dementiae "That dogs

bark at me as I halt by them" the word
Kierkegaard uses to describe writing is "desultory"

meaning for him leaping from one point to
another to illuminate the subject

from all sides or in order that the un-
intelligibility might be broken

down into its several parts in his
hilarious lyrical treatise *Fear*

and Trembling was a necessary method
desultorius literally of a

circus rider who leaps from horse to horse
his notebooks too show his obsession with hats

which erupted after he broke off
his engagement with Regina hats

either represented his fear
of sex or were an ornament calculated

to distract people from noticing
his hump evenings when he would promenade

in front of the opera house in a top hat
I do not remember SK's auditory

hallucination that convinced him
to publish his *Sickness* book but in it

is a sentence all men should take to heart
"by relating itself to its own self

and by willing to be itself the self
is grounded transparently in the power

which posited it" the formula which
describes the self when despair is completely

eradicated—exactly like the
entire long-worn hat situation where hat

and head are one *Ah!* now I know why
I am here just as the yarmulkah is where

it is as Rabbi Nachman made clear when
in the middle of an ecstatic prayer

he whipped the yarmulkah off his head and cursed
God for not giving him money to fix

the leaky roof of his synagogue
(a communal hat) cursed Him for his wis-

dom His sleepless need to continue this
fiasco *Life on Earth* to His refusal

to eliminate the seductive truth
of "Faith is a miracle, and yet no

man is excluded from it; for that in which
all human life is unified is passion,

and faith is a passion." thus torturing
each one of us by pointing to the highest:

"teleological suspension of the
ethical" in moods like this he'd recite

(to himself) his translation of
Baudelaire's suppressed sonnet Black Evening:

"Nipples at twilight glow like pink closed buds,
stiff, rich with passion. When I put my mouth

around one, bite it, suck it, feel your crotch
grow wetter all I want is your cold mouth

on my cock, sucking the tip, nuzzling it,
then I go down on you until you come,

until I feel the wet silk of your pussy
change into a greedy innocent mouth

and you demand my cock and I refuse,
you lift your skirt, naked under it, show

me your prime tight ass so all I can do
is hold my cock up to your face while you

kiss it and I can't stop fingering you
until you come, and then I slip my cock in."

to counteract the fury that drove him
to his knees unlike the hatband of a fine

old sweat-stained fedora snug weightless as love
you don't know you have it on from the first

moment you slip it down onto your head
locking the door behind you with a deadbolt

key strolling through the fluffy lush carpet
of cherry blossoms fallen from your tree

then down the hill into the burning city
the sad hatlessness of "nothing to be

resolved" clear fire in your belly
like the detached grief you feel when death

a friend's death is upon you "My soul
cleaveth unto the dust: quicken thou me

according to thy word." "For I am become
like a bottle in the smoke…" I wonder

what Baudelaire's prose poem *Death* would have
been written even near his own the *telluric*

dismal bedpans and drugs (civil service
deputy chief clerk's salary between 2,000

and 2,700 francs CB is paid 2,400
from the interest on his capital) his

walking-stick tied to a button-hole
a purely etymological poem

first fragments of it humming in his head
ende enti end Latin *ante* Greek *anti*

against the part of an area that lies
at the boundary a point that marks the extent

of something the point where something ceases
to exist the extreme or last part lengthwise

the terminal unit of something spatial
i. e . to become space itself is death

to take up no space just ask yourself
as the theory of quantum electro–

dynamics describes Nature as absurd
from the point of view of common sense

and agrees fully with the experiment
can you accept nature as she is—absurd

"a kind of lace snood *(maintenon)* fitted
onto the hat and tied on above the ribbons

the little toque has a pompon or a wing
a *Longueville* hat is a Lavailiere

with a single feather which floats and flaps
in the wind coolness light whiteness the

sparkling colors of a flower-bed what
sadness there is in this solitary

frivolity a distressing emotion
of foolish ruin a monument to

gaiety standing in a desert" but if
you could only take this last Baudelaire note

for The Elegy on Hats and use it
to see death as "The suburban milliner,

pale, anaemic, milk coffee, like an old
tobacconist with bad breath" you might pity

death love the stranger kneeling in the window
shaping cloth over the wooden dummy

head size 7 just right for a customer who walks in
and yells "Beautiful! It fits! I'll take it!"

NOTES

1.

[E] A hat. Smooth surface.

A cap. Folded or bubbling surface.

The pass (from the spot which no longer sits on the head.)

The part at the back is called the crown or dome, or the lining, when it is fluted.

Bonnet strings. Fasteners or little ribbons.

Feathers, marabous or aigrettes.

Head bands, of feathers or flowers.

A *maintenon*, a kind of lace snood, fitted onto the hat and tied on above the ribbons.

A *Mary Stuart*, a form in which the peak is very low, a Sarrasin or ogival shape.

A *Lavallière* (gone out of fashion) with two feathers meeting behind.

Russian hat. An aigrette.

The little toque has a pompon or a wing.

A flower (rose) placed on a *Marie-Louise*.

A *Marinière* hat, with a bouquet.

A *Longueville* hat is a Lavallière with a single feather which floats and flaps in the wind.

A Scottish hat, in poplin with squares, has a rosette, a silver clasp, and an eagle's or a raven's feather.

Ornaments: puffs, ruffs, bias cuts, borders.

The furnishing of a fashion shop:

Curtains in muslin or silk of a uniform white colour. Divans.

Looking glass, a smooth, mobile surface. Oval, inclined mirrors.

Large oval table, with a long-legged hatstand. A fairies' laboratory. A clean task.

General appearance: coolness, light, whiteness, the sparkling colours
    of a flower-bed.
Ribbons, frills, tulle, gauze, muslin, feathers, etc...
The hats inspire thoughts of faces, and look like a gallery of faces.
For each hat, because of its character, evokes a face and lets the
    mind's eye see it. Guillotined heads.
What sadness there is in this solitary frivolity! A distressing feeling
    of foolish ruin. A monument to gaiety standing in a desert.
Frivolity in abandon.
The suburban milliner, pale, anaemic, milk coffee, like an old
    tobacconist.
A distressed feeling.

(—from Baudelaire's posthumous [Plays and Notes])

2.

My impulse to imagine Baudelaire's unwritten *The Great Prayer* in
part 12 of *The Elegy on Hats* led me to use all of *Sleeping Woman* as
his *Prayer*. *Sleeping Woman* is a 1200′ line of words stenciled and
glazed in 1991 atop the 30′ wide stone retaining wall between the
grassbank and the water of Kelly Drive along the Schuylkill River
in Philadelphia. My collaborator was the American artist Tom
Chimes. The project was commissioned by The Fairmount Park Art
Association, whose director, Penny Bach, made the entire enterprise
possible.

ABOUT STEPHEN BERG

On the same day as this volume, Berg is publishing *Rimbaud: Versions & Inventions* with Sheep Meadow Press. Other books published by Stephen Berg include *Halo* (Sheep Meadow Press), *Clouded Sky: Poems by Miklos Radnoti* (Sheep Meadow Press), *The Daughters, Grief, With Akhmatova at the Black Gates, In It, The Steel Cricket,* and *Crow with No Mouth: Ikkyū.* He is the founder and coeditor of the *American Poetry Review,* and the recipient of Rockefeller, Guggenheim, NEA, Dietrich Foundation, and Pew fellowships.